Do Your Ears Hang Low?

and Other Silly Songs

Illustrated by Pamela Cote

Cartwheel
·B·O·O·K·S· ®

SCHOLASTIC INC.

New York Toronto London Auckland Sydney

ISBN 0-590-20305-3

Copyright © 1995 by Scholastic Inc.
Illustrations copyright © 1995 by Pamela Cote.
All rights reserved. Published by Scholastic Inc.
CARTWHEEL BOOKS and the CARTWHEEL BOOKS logo
are registered trademarks of Scholastic Inc.

12 11 10 9 8 7 6 5 4   5 6 7 8 9/9 0/0

Printed in the U.S.A.   24

First Scholastic printing, March 1995

Contents

Oh, Susanna!

Oh, I come from Alabama
With a banjo on my knee;
I'm going to Lou'siana,
My true love for to see.

It rained all night the day I left;
The weather it was dry.
The sun so hot I froze to death;
Susanna, don't you cry.

Oh, Susanna!
Now don't you cry for me;
I come from Alabama
With a banjo on my knee.

I had a dream the other night;
When everything was still.
I thought I saw Susanna,
A-coming down the hill.

The color rose was in her cheek;
A tear was in her eye.
I said to her, "Susanna,
Susanna, don't you cry."

6

Oh, Susanna!
Now don't you cry for me;
I come from Alabama
With a banjo on my knee.

Do Your Ears Hang Low?

Do your ears hang low?
Do they wobble to-and-fro?
Can you tie them in a knot;
Can you tie them in a bow?
Can you throw them over your shoulder,
Like a continental soldier;
Do your ears hang low?

(Sing it again! This time, sing about a
different body part for a really silly song!
Try this: Does your *nose* hang low? or,
Do your *toes* hang low?)

Turkey in the Straw

As I was a-going down the road
With a tired team and a heavy load,
I cracked my whip and the leader sprung;
I said, "Day-day" to the wagon tongue.

Turkey in the straw,
Haw, haw, haw, haw.
Turkey in the hay,
Hay, hay, hay, hay.

Roll 'em up, twist 'em up,
High tuck-a haw;
And hit 'em with a tune called
"Turkey in the Straw."

Oh, I went out to milk and I didn't know how.
I milked the goat instead of the cow.
A monkey sitting on a pile of straw
A-winking his eye at his mother-in-law.

Turkey in the straw
Haw, haw, haw, haw.
Turkey in the hay,
Hay, hay, hay, hay.

Roll 'em up, twist 'em up,
High tuck-a haw;
And hit 'em with a tune called
"Turkey in the Straw."

13

Little Bunny Foo Foo

Little bunny foo foo,
Hopping through the forest;
Scooping up the field mice
And bopping them on the head.

Down came the Good Fairy,
And she said,
"Little bunny foo foo,
I don't want to see you
Scooping up the field mice
And bopping them on the head.
I'll give you three chances,
And if you don't behave,
I'll turn you into a GOON."

But the next day...
Little bunny foo foo,
Hopping through the forest;
Scooping up the field mice
And bopping them on the head.

Down came the Good Fairy,
And she said,
"Little bunny foo foo,
I don't want to see you
Scooping up the field mice
And bopping them on the head.
I'll give you two more chances,
And if you don't behave,
I'll turn you into a GOON."

But the very next day…
Little bunny foo foo,
Hopping through the forest;
Scooping up the field mice
And bopping them on the head.

Down came the Good Fairy,
And she said,
"Little bunny foo foo,
I don't want to see you
Scooping up the field mice
And bopping them on the head.
I'll give you one more chance,
And if you don't behave,
I'll turn you into a GOON."

But the very next day…
Little bunny foo foo,
Hopping through the forest;
Scooping up the field mice
And bopping them on the head.

Once again, the Good Fairy appeared,
And, boy, was she angry!

She said,
"Little bunny foo foo,
I gave you three chances
to behave, and you blew it!"
Suddenly there was a great rumbling,
Then a bright flash, and *POOF!*
Little bunny foo foo wasn't
A bunny anymore;
She was a GOON!

And do you all know the moral of this story?
Hare today; GOON tomorrow!

Kookaburra

Kookaburra sits in the old gum tree,
Merry, merry king of the bush is he.
Laugh, Kookaburra,
Laugh, Kookaburra,
Gay your life must be.

Kookaburra sits in the old gum tree,
Eating all the gumdrops he can see,
Stop, Kookaburra,
Stop, Kookaburra,
Leave just one for me.

Mairzy Doats

Mairzy doats,
And dozy doats,
And little lamzy divy.
A kiddle-lee divy too,
Wouldn't you?

Mares eats oats,
And does eat oats,
And little lambs eat ivy.
A kid will eat ivy too,
Wouldn't you?

Boom! Boom! Ain't it great to be crazy?
Boom! Boom! Ain't it great to be crazy?
Giddy and foolish all day long.
Boom! Boom! Ain't it great to be crazy?

A horse and a flea and three blind mice
Sat on a curbstone eating rice.
The horse he slipped and fell on the flea.
"Oh, no!" said the flea.
"There's a horse on me!"

24

Boom! Boom! Ain't it great to be crazy?
Boom! Boom! Ain't it great to be crazy?
Giddy and foolish all day long.
Boom! Boom! Ain't it great to be crazy?

Eli, Eli, he sells socks;
A quarter a pair, or a dollar a box.
The longer you wear them,
The shorter they get.
You put them in the water
And they don't get wet!

Boom! Boom! Ain't it great to be crazy?
Boom! Boom! Ain't it great to be crazy?
Giddy and foolish all day long.
Boom! Boom! Ain't it great to be crazy?

The Fly Has Married the Bumblebee

Fiddle-dee-dee, fiddle-dee-dee,
The fly has married the bumblebee.

Says the fly, says he,
"Will you marry me,
And live with me,
Sweet bumblebee?"

Fiddle-dee-dee, fiddle-dee-dee,
The fly has married the bumblebee.

Says the bee, says she,
"I'll live under your wing,
And you'll never know
I carry a sting."

Fiddle-dee-dee, fiddle-dee-dee,
The fly has married the bumblebee.

So when the parson beetle
Joined the pair,
They both went out
To take the air.

Fiddle-dee-dee, fiddle-dee-dee,
The fly has married the bumblebee.

And the flies did buzz,
And the bells did ring.
Did ever you hear
So merry a thing?

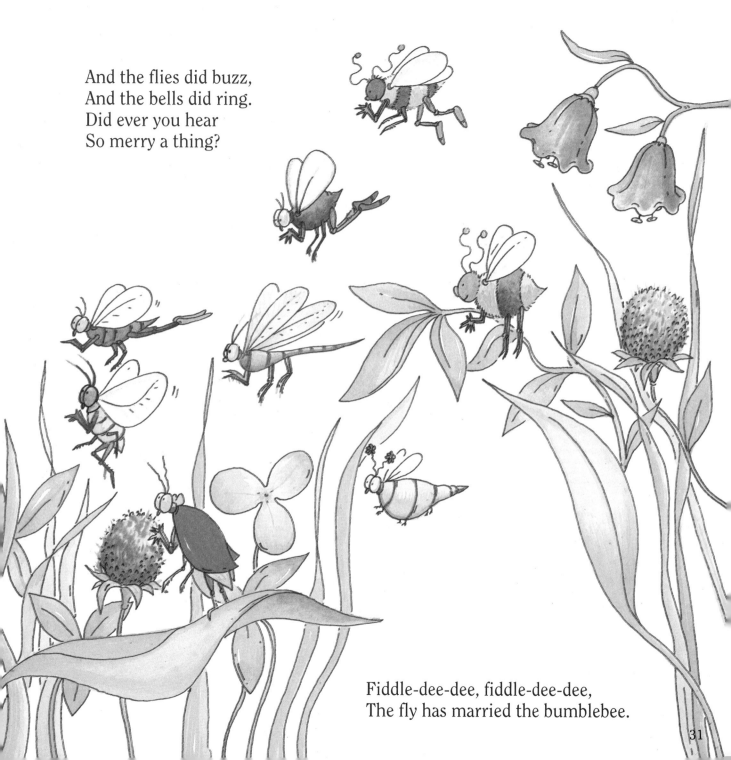

Fiddle-dee-dee, fiddle-dee-dee,
The fly has married the bumblebee.

Shoo Fly

Shoo, fly, don't bother me.
Shoo, fly, don't bother me.
Shoo, fly, don't bother me.
For I belong to somebody.

I feel, I feel, I feel,
I feel like a morning star.
I feel, I feel, I feel,
I feel like a morning star.

So, shoo, fly, don't bother me.
Shoo, fly, don't bother me.
Shoo, fly, don't bother me.
For I belong to somebody.